T

Of Faith

by
Norvel Hayes

(Volume number four of a nine part series on The Gifts Of The Spirit.)

HARRISON HOUSE
P.O. Box 35035
Tulsa, Okla. 74135

". . . to another faith by the same Spirit"
I Corinthians 12:9

ISBN 0-89274-142-2
Copyright © 1980 by Norvel Hayes
Printed in the United States of America

Table of Contents

1

For All Spirit-filled Believers

If you are a believer and have been baptized in the Holy Ghost, all of the nine gifts of the Spirit *should* be operating through you. I said they should be. And they will be, if you know how to listen to the Holy Spirit and know what He's trying to get across to you. The gifts of the Spirit are so important.

What are the gifts of the Spirit anyway? **The nine gifts of the Spirit are God's spiritual weapons that He's given to the church.**

Now remember, God is a Spirit. The devil is a spirit. You are living on the earth where the Holy Spirit and the devil live. But this world has been turned over to the devil. He took it over because man would not listen to God. Rebellion against God, caused the devil to take it over.

Since that time, if you are going to get any information from heaven, it's got to be through the Word and the Spirit. Listen to God. He is talking to you. Now remember, this is not just some Bible story, God is talking to you—if you're born again.

2
Don't Be Ignorant

This is the 12th chapter of I Corinthians. *"Now concerning spiritual gifts, brethren, I would not have you ignorant"* (verse 1).

God doesn't want you to be ignorant of the gifts of the Spirit. You might say, "They don't all operate through me. Why don't I have them?"

It's because you're ignorant of them. Now, I didn't say **you** were an ignorant person. I said YOU ARE IGNORANT OF THE GIFTS. You don't understand how they operate.

You might say, "Why don't they operate through me?"

Basically because you've never studied or heard too much on the 12th chapter of I Corinthians. Besides that, you've probably had a bunch of junk in your spirit that you got from the church you went to when you were a child. You will have to ask the Holy Spirit to burn all that out before you can get this.

If you don't believe that, listen to this verse right here. *"Ye know that ye were gentiles carried away unto these dumb idols even as ye were led"* (verse 2).

Many of you, your father and mother led you to church when you were little, but you went to some old, cold, dumb church. But, see, you didn't know it. They didn't even have healing services. They made fun of tongues, and didn't have any miracles. They just floated along and had Sunday School class. God doesn't float along! Do you understand that?

God is all powerful and He wants to manifest himself and give you everything you need. He will if you believe it.

The reason the gifts of the Spirit don't operate and aren't given out through very many churches, is because they don't believe it. When they start teaching on it, preaching on it, and believing it, then it will come into manifestation. It will be given out by the Holy Ghost that lives inside of them.

You can't fight the Bible and get God to give you anything. The Holy Ghost does in the congregation what goes out from behind the pulpit. That's what He does. I mean, HE DOES IT!

God says to you and me, *"Wherefore, I give you to understand, that no man speaking by the Spirit of God calleth Jesus accursed: and that no man can say that Jesus is the Lord, but by the Holy Ghost. Now there are diversities of gifts, but the same Spirit. And there are differences of administrations, but it is the same Lord. And there are diversities of operations, but the same God which worketh all in all. But the manifestation of the Spirit is given to every man to profit withal"* (verse 3-7).

Now many of you didn't know that. "Why, Brother Norvel, I don't have discerning of spirits; I don't have the word of wisdom operating through me. I don't have the gift of faith operating through me where supernatural power comes upon me. I don't have this and I don't have that."

Listen closely to the seventh verse. *"But the manifestation of the Spirit is given to every man to profit withal* (Is given to every man, every man, EVERY MAN)."

Does every man include you?

You can have it if you want it. You have to believe it.

8

"For to one is given by the Spirit the word of wisdom; to another the word of knowledge by the same Spirit; To another faith by the same Spirit; to another the gifts of healing by the same Spirit; To another the working of miracles; to another prophecy; to another discerning of spirits; to another divers kinds of tongues; to another the interpretation of tongues: But all these worketh that one and the selfsame Spirit, dividing to every man severally as he will. For as the body is one, and hath many members, and all the members of that one body, being many, are one body: so also is Christ" (verse 8-12).

"But now hath God set the members every one of them in the body, as it hath pleased him. And if they were all one member, where were the body? But now are they many members, yet but one body. And the eye cannot say to the hand, I have no need of thee: nor again the head to the feet, I have no need of you" (verse 18-21).

I want you to know, and I want you to get it inside of you real good, solid and strong, that every one of the gifts of the Spirit is just as important as the other when that particular gift is needed. Every one of the gifts of the Spirit is a matter of life and death on a particular day for you in your life in a particular situation. You can't cut one of them short or say this one is more important than that one. No it's not. Every one of them is just as important as every other one at the time that one is needed.

Now there are some of them that operate very closely together. The gift of faith, many times, is the twin brother to the gift of healing. It could be twin to the working of miracles. The word of wisdom is like a twin brother to the word of knowledge. But they operate completely differently.

9

3

Different Kinds of Faith

There are three power gifts: the gift of faith, the gifts of healing, and the gift of working of miracles. God is powerful! God is so powerful He speaks worlds into existence. God is all powerful.

Just know this, if you're crippled and sitting there today reading this, God has power to make your leg normal and stretch it out. He has the power.

You say, "I wish He'd give it to me." If you're crippled or you need that, I know you do; I know you wish He'd give it to you. And He will, if you will get into the gifts of the Spirit and believe them. Get the faith and believe it. Get the right kind of confession and believe it. God will manifest himself and give you anything.

Your faith has to pass the test in the book of Hebrews. You can't believe God any way you want to and get God to manifest himself. You have to believe God according to the Bible.

"Now faith is the substance of things hoped for, the evidence of things not seen" (Hebrews 11:1).

I'm talking about the regular faith, the Hebrews-kind of faith, not the gift of faith. The power of faith doesn't ever see anything from the time of the prayer until the day the manifestation comes and you are jumping and leaping and praising God. **The power of faith doesn't ever see the pitfalls between the prayer and the manifestation.** The manifestation may come *five minutes* after you pray, but it might come *five years* after you pray.

If your eyes of faith ever see the condition, and ever dwell upon the condition, it is not the power of faith and it won't work for you. You can't give attention to anything in regular faith except what the Bible has promised you.

You have to take God's words and speak them out of your mouth. When you take God's words that come out of His mouth, and speak them out of your mouth, then God hears them and manifests himself to you. That is, UNLESS YOU WAVER.

You say, "I waited for three or four months and it never did come to pass; so I just got tired of waiting."

That shows that you are ignorant of the Bible. *Your spirit doesn't possess patience.* God tells you in the first chapter of the book of James, that unless your spirit possesses patience, you're not going to get anything.

You might say, "I didn't know that was in there."

That's too bad, you should have studied it. It's in there. God put it in there for you. Study it and you'll find it's there. You have to be a good student of the Scriptures. You can't read the Bible whenever you want to. You have to burn the midnight oil sometimes. You didn't get your high school diploma by believing those books any way you wanted to, or by being nonchalant about it. You didn't pass. That's not the way you got your high school diploma. You are not going to get your healing that way either. You're going to get your healing from God or whatever you need from God, exactly the same way you got your high school diploma, and there are no short cuts.

You say, "I'm going to a healing meeting and let somebody lay hands on me so God will heal me."

That won't last long.

You say, "Will I get my healing if I go there?"

Probably.

"Will I keep it?"

No. You might keep it a year. You might keep it a month. I have known people to keep it for two or three years. But you'll lose it. If you don't get interested in the Bible, and build a foundation of your believing on the Bible, that thing will come back upon you. Why? Because the devil is not dead.

I know a woman, a good friend of mine, a pastor's wife, and yet she was dying of cancer 25 years ago. Jesus walked into her room and healed her and she has been healed ever since. The devil's been trying to give her cancer for 25 years. She won't receive it. Symptoms of cancer come back, but she has faith enough in God's Word that she will get flat on the floor, and pray herself through the doubt and unbelief, and the smog and fog from hell.

Every six months or so the devil will come and try to kill her with cancer; but she won't receive it. She prays until everything leaves her. She prays herself into the glory of God. She prays until God's healing power comes and surges down through her and removes all symptoms from her. She prays until that happens. That is what you call *Hebrews kind of faith*—**you believe that God means what He says.** Right now! Faith is the substance! She believes that her faith is the substance to health. And brother, she gets it, too. I know her personally. But that is not the gift of faith. You can learn to do that on your own.

There are all kinds of faith. Let me point out some other kinds of faith to you.

A farmer has faith. He sows his seed and believes it is going to come up. That is faith.

13

You are standing on a busy street corner, and cars are coming down the street. You look up and see a little light up there, and it is red. It turns green. You start walking across. You think the cars are going to stop, and most of the time they do. But you have faith to walk across the street.

You have faith when you put your money in the bank, that the bank is not going to steal it. You have faith that they are not going to put it in somebody else's account. You believe they are going to put it in your account. Most of the time they do. Sometimes they don't. You have faith in them.

Why don't you have the same kind of faith in God's Word?

4

The Gift of Faith in Manifestation in the Bible

The gift of faith is a *gift of power*. I want you to understand how the gift of power works and why God will give it to you.

God gives a believer a gift of power because there is something that He wants to do. It is always to bless somebody or help somebody. Or, God can give a believer the gift of power to stop something that is evil.

Let me point out a couple of Bible men, that had the gift of faith operating through them. These men are in the Old Testament. The gift of faith was in the Old Testament.

Daniel had the gift of faith operating in his life. He was a man of God. (See Daniel chapter 6.) When they put him in the lions' den, he was thoroughly convinced that the lions would not bite him. *Lions lay down!* And of course in the morning he was still there. The angel had come and shut the lions' mouths. God's power came and he knew it. He had the faith. He wasn't a nervous wreck when he went in there.

The average Christian, that didn't know anything about the things of the Spirit, and didn't know God that well, would have been a nervous wreck. God doesn't answer nervous prayers, so they would have been eaten up.

If your spirit doesn't have any *patience*, you'd just have been eaten up. God cannot override the Word to give you something that is in the Bible, even though He wants to. He hates to see you miss it, and not get it. But He can't override the Bible. When God says your spirit needs to be possessing patience, that is exactly what He means.

You say, "Well, I'm nervous all the time, Brother Norvel. I'm nervous and I don't have much patience. I guess I'm just an old doubter."

I tell people like that, "Shut up! Don't say that! The devil will kill you."

I'm trying to save their life that's all. Some people's mouth kills them. They just go around saying dumb things. The devil hears them.

God can't help you when you talk wrong. If you talk the Word, God can help you. If you don't, the devil hears you. You open the door of doubt and the devil comes in. He'll try to mess you up in every way. But you can get God's power working for you through the gift of faith.

The gift of faith came upon Samson. He had more power than any human being recorded in the Bible. But God gave it to Samson **when he needed it**. He gave it to him. (See Judges 15:14-15.)

A whole army was going to get him; but he just killed the whole bunch, hundreds of them, by himself, with the jawbone of a donkey. Brother, that's power! That's power! The Spirit of God came upon him and changed him into another man, completely. He had more of God's power than anybody that I know of, as far as things like that are concerned. But it is a gift of the Spirit.

God's a Spirit who lives in heaven. How does He operate through you?

He operates through you, by the Holy Spirit that lives inside of you.

When God sees that you are available, He will give you the gift of faith: *the amount of power to get the job done, which is always to help somebody, or help you, or do away with evil.*

God gave that to Samson to stop those men from killing him. God didn't want Samson killed.

God gave Daniel the amount of power he needed on him, so the lions COULDN'T eat him. They could eat anybody else, but not Daniel. God's Holy Presence came in there where the lions were.

(If Samson had been in there, he would have made hamburger meat all over the place; he'd have killed the whole bunch of them.)

But Daniel had enough steadfastness about him that the lions just laid down quiet like kittens. God gave him the power to do that.

The gift of faith is a gift of power to get the job done in whatever situation that you are in at that particular time. It is a gift of power. God doesn't give you ALL His power, and different times He gives you different amounts of power. *He only gives you the amount of power you need to get THAT JOB DONE.*

5
To Help Someone

Let me explain how the *gift of faith* operates through a believer's life. The first time it ever operated in my life, was for the benefit of somebody else.

Who?

A Spirit-filled Christian woman, to keep her from dying.

Jesus loves His family. He doesn't want you to die of diseases. He doesn't want the devil coming and putting diseases on you and killing you. That is not God's will for you. It happens to people many times. But God doesn't want it.

God has the power to give you healing. But sometimes it takes the gift of faith, as authority, *to get somebody to BELIEVE that.* Sometimes the gift of healing follows the gift of faith.

Sometimes diseases beat people down. I understand why they do, perfectly. They get a disease and they don't have faith to get healed. The disease beats them down day after day, month after month, year after year. After a while, in the natural, they get so used to being sick, that they kind of give up. What comes, let it come. They just get beaten down.

That is the way this woman was. She started getting sick in her stomach. Then she had trouble with her breathing. It kept getting worse. Her husband had to take her to Florida all the time. He had to keep her in Florida, six months sometimes, and let her sit out in the sun. It didn't help her stomach any, but it helped her breathing a little. She could live.

19

This woman and her husband were both Spirit-filled and loved God. I was scheduled to be the speaker at the FGBMFI chapter where the husband was an officer. The wife's name is Helen. She played the piano for conventions and things like that. God was wanting to use her mightily.

I spoke that night and then gave the invitation. She was one of the first ones in line to be prayed for. She came for healing. I prayed for her and for all the rest of them down the line. When I got through praying, I was just standing there. The Spirit of God was working with some of them. Some of them were praising the Lord. Some of them were walking back to their seats.

I looked up where she was sitting. She looked so sad. I didn't know what was happening to me, but the moment I looked on her, I began to see her healed. Power came on me! And I got mad at her. I didn't, but God did. Sometimes the Lord will get mad at you.

It's good for you that the Lord will get mad at you. Sometimes you get in the habit of thinking one way and you can't think any other way. God wants to change your way of thinking.

God got mad at her because she was doing that. She should have been rejoicing because I laid hands on her for healing. She should have been operating in the book of Hebrews.

She should have been walking up and down the church, or at least sitting back in her seat saying, "Thank God, I'm healed! Thank you, Jesus, I'm healed! Glory to God, I'm healed!"

But she wasn't. She was sitting there with her head down. She looked like she was getting ready to die. I never saw such a sad look on anybody's face.

I looked at her, and the power came on me. It was like everybody else in the place just disappeared from me. I knew they were there, but I couldn't care less. The gift of faith dropped on me, and I could not have cared less what anybody thought.

I walked over to her, and I said, "HELEN!"

She looked up at me.

I said, "WHAT ARE YOU GOING TO DO? SIT HERE AND LET THE DEVIL KILL YOU? WHY DON'T YOU RISE UP? I PRAYED FOR YOU IN JESUS' NAME ONE TIME! THAT IS ALL YOU NEED, HELEN. DO YOU UNDERSTAND THAT? YOU ARE HEALED! BY HIS STRIPES YOU ARE HEALED! WHY DON'T YOU RISE UP HELEN? WHY DON'T YOU RISE UP HELEN? LET GOD HEAL YOU! DON'T SIT THERE AND LET THE DEVIL KILL YOU! WHY DON'T YOU RISE UP, HELEN! WHY DON'T YOU RISE UP!"

While I was doing that she was looking at me. I did that for about 30 seconds. I kept saying that.

All of a sudden she looked at me and said, "YEAH, YEAH, YEAH, OKAY!!! NORVEL! OKAY, NORVEL! YEAH! YEAH! YEAH!"

The power came like the wind, and left like the wind. The power wasn't on me anymore. God changed me so quickly and He restored me back to my normal self, just as quickly. It was like the bat of an eye.

Then, *the same power that was on me, was on her.* She was standing there screaming the victory just like I had been screaming at her. She was screaming, "I'M HEALED."

I was standing there with no power. You know what happens don't you, if you obey God? Immediately, up in your mind, (that is where the devil operates—in your mind) the devil starts in.

He said to me, "You're nuts! You're crazy! You're a fanatic! They'll never invite you to speak here again, you crazy thing! What are you screaming at that woman for like that? That is not nice." The devil is cunning. He will come to you just so slick and smooth. That was my first time. I thought, Oh, what did I do?

The devil said, "They will never invite you back here to speak. You have just closed the doors for your ministry, because this will get out all over the country, and you've had it. You will not get any more invitations, you dummy! You crazy thing! You're getting too wild, you're supposed to be nice."

I thought, Oh, God, what did I do? I was ashamed to look at the people. But I did look at them. Some of them were looking at me and some of them were looking at her.

She was still standing there screaming, "I'M HEALED." *It went from me into her.* But I didn't know that until about a week later.

There was a convention a week later not very far away. I thought I would go up one day, see who was speaking and enjoy the service. I just walked into the auditorium. There were several hundred people there. Helen was playing the piano.

When she saw me come in, she stopped playing the piano and jumped off the stage. She ran down the aisle to where I was, and said, "Brother Norvel, I'm healed. I'm healed completely. Everything has disappeared. I went out that night and ate a T-bone steak, and I digested it. It's the first time I've digested food in six months. I've been eating baby food for six months. I have eaten anything I wanted to since that night,

Brother Norvel. Everything has disappeared from me. I breathe real good, and my stomach is completely healed. Look at my face, I'm getting my color back. My cheeks are already turning rosy. I've gained about nine pounds since that night. Norvel, do you remember me? Do you remember that night, when you were screaming at me?"

I said, "Yeah, honey, I remember when I was screaming at you."

She said, "You probably don't know what happened. While you were screaming at me, I was just sitting there. While you were screaming at me that power started coming from you and into me. That power that went into me, caused me to be strong enough, and bold enough, to start confessing my healing—boldly. *When I started confessing my healing boldly, I got healed.* All the afflictions disappeared!"

The *gift of faith* is what did it. I know the gift of healing followed it when she started confessing her healing, but the gift of faith changed me into another person to make her think differently.

The gift of faith caused a woman who had been eating only baby food for six months, to start eating normally and not die! I don't mean three days later; I mean right then—in a few minutes.

God gave me the power to talk to her like that so she could start believing the Bible and rise up against that thing.

You have to rise up against the devil. I don't care what kind of works the devil gives, you have to rise up against the devil. Rise up against him!

23

6

To Stop the Works of Hell

God gave me great favor one time by the *gift of faith* operating through me.

I was speaking in a prison out at Canyon City, Colorado. They had a bunch of killings in the penitentiary. Four or five boys had escaped from death row. The guards shot about three of them trying to climb the walls.

They had had several stabbings and deaths on the inside, with knives they couldn't find. The guards would go up to a prisoner's cell and he'd be lying there dead. Somebody had been stabbed at the mess hall, too. They'd tried to find the knife, but couldn't. They couldn't find who was committing the murders and stabbing the people.

I'd been working with a fellow that was in the penitentiary. He told them. "I know a fellow that will come out here and speak to them if you will invite him."

"Really?"

"Yeah, he'd come inside the walls here and speak to them, if you would invite him."

They said, "See if you can get him."

So he wrote me a letter and asked me if I would come. I said, "Yeah, if they want me to."

I flew to Denver, and some fellows took me down there to Canyon City, Colorado. I went in and they talked to me. They said, "I guess you already know that it could be dangerous. Would you be willing to counsel with the men after the meeting?"

I said, "Yeah, I will."

"We fixed up a little buffet of food. After you get through speaking to the prisoners, you'll walk across the yard with them, go in the mess hall, mingle with them and have refreshments. You can stay in there for about an hour, if you are willing to go in. We're going to tell you right now, that it could get dangerous. It could cost you your life," they said.

I said, "If I can help them, I'll go."

So they introduced me. I got up on the stage, and hundreds of prisoners came in. (I was going to speak to them first and eat with them afterwards.)

I got up there and started talking about Jesus. *Boy, that really went over like a lead balloon.* I started talking about Jesus and they started laughing at me. I don't mean one or two of them, I mean they all started laughing at me and pointing at me. I was trying to talk to them about Jesus, and they just kept laughing and pointing towards me.

I just acted like I didn't see them. I had to shut my mind off from them, which is easier said than done. I just kept on, and acted like I had a one-track mind.

That lasted about 20 or 25 minutes, until God got tired of it. God gave them every chance in the world to shut up, but they didn't do it.

All of a sudden, POWER fell on me! **I'M TALKING ABOUT SUPERNATURAL POWER.** I wasn't a regular Bible teacher any more. I wasn't standing there any more just speaking with authority, and teaching the Bible. **POWER came on me!** Glory to God! He changed me into another man.

They looked like objects to me. One of the big laughers and hecklers was sitting there on the front. I was on the stage. (From the natural I wouldn't have done this. I might do it with a bunch of teenagers. You know what I mean. I'm fooling with killers that already have 200 or 300 years. I've been warned not to make them mad.) I can see they are already mad. They are so mad, they are laughing about it, making fun.

The devil said to me, "You've got a nice meal coming up and you're going to have to eat with this bunch."

God got tired of them making fun of me.

What did He do for you?

The gift of faith came upon me.

What's that?

It's a gift of power.

You mean God gave you His power?

Not all of it. Just a small amount of it. *God gave me the amount of power I needed to get the job done at this particular moment.* He gave me the words to say.

He'll not only give you the power to do it, He'll give you the words to say.

The gift of faith can jerk you out of your thinking and make you think another way. All of the prisoners were sitting there thinking one way, and making fun of me. I had spoken in prisons before, and had hecklers and such, but not anything like that. I never faced anything that severe before.

All of a sudden power came on me. I just backed away from the pulpit they had on stage there. Then I walked over to the side, and God began to give me words. *I began to see the works of hell.*

I looked at them, straight in the face, and said, "What are you fellows laughing at me for? I'm not in here. You are the ones that are in here, you dummies! I came in here to give you life, so you could go to heaven and live forever; and you're sitting there and laughing and making fun and heckling. God doesn't like it. God knows where you are sitting! He knows who you are! He knows exactly what happened to you! But you don't even know, you are so ignorant!

"Now you, sitting there, you're so dumb you don't even know why you raped that woman. You're 24 years old and you raped a woman 60 years old. You don't even know why you did that! You got 65 years.

"You over here, you don't even know why you robbed that bank. You're sitting here with 25 years, and you're so dumb, you don't even know what made you rob the bank.

"You, why did you shoot that man? You don't even know why you shot that man! You're so ignorant, you don't even know why you are in here.

"But then they closed the doors on you, and they marched you down the long corridor, kicked you and shoved you into the cell, and you said, 'I wish I hadn't done that.' Well, big deal! You're so dumb! You don't even know what made you commit the crime! But I know! I know exactly what put you in here.

"Nearly every one of you sitting there, like little lambs, is thinking, when I get out, I'm going to be better. No you're not going to be better, you evil hard-hearted rascal! You're going to be meaner! That same demon from hell that put you in here this time, will put you in here again! Do you understand that? He will put you in here again. 87% of the prisoners that get out, come back again. They say, 'Oh, I'll never come back

28

again.' The record says that 87% of you will come back again. I came to tell you how to stay out forever! Do you understand that? Now I want you to sit there and be quiet!"

I never heard another noise. I never heard another laugh or anything from the moment I first opened my mouth and started when God's power fell on me supernaturally.

I just told them, "I love you whether you like it or don't like it. God loves you whether you like it or don't like it. He wants to tell you exactly what to do to get out of here and stay out forever! You have a right to be a free human being, and not to be under the bondage of the devil.

"The devil himself got into you. I know why: you started running with the wrong crowd. That's how you got to thinking like that. Your thinking is screwed up! You let Jesus touch you and He'll get your thinking straightened out."

I just kept on going for ten minutes. I guess I didn't teach anymore, I started preaching. God's power fell on me for about ten minutes and gave it to them.

Then I said, "Bow your heads! I'm going to pray for you."

They bowed their heads.

"Jesus, I know you love these men! Touch their hearts. I ask you to do it. You don't want these men in this prison, Jesus. You didn't put them in here. You want them to be citizens. You want these boys that aren't married to get married. You don't want them to fool around with each other. You want them to get married to a girl, have children, have a family, be normal."

As I was praying for them, God's power came in. They broke and started crying. The Lord just moved in there so strong.

I said, "The state of Colorado won't allow me to give an invitation. I'd like to put my arms around each one of you and pray for you, but they won't let me. Every one of you that know you've done wrong, but you're not proud of it, and you believe Jesus is real and He loves you; you'd like Jesus to show you He loves you; you'd like to give your life to Him and say yes to Him, and stop fighting Him, hold up your right hand."

Hands began to go up all over the prison. I got them to repeat a sinner's prayer. I dismissed them.

I told them, "I'm walking with you. We are going over to have some food together. If I can answer any of your questions, feel free to ask me. I know what the power of the devil is just as you do. Many people out there have done worse things than you've done, but you got caught and they didn't."

The guy in front, the big heckler, broke and started crying. He got up out of his seat, and came up to the stage after I dismissed them. His lips were quivering and his face was sad.

He walked up to me and said, "Mister, I'm sorry I laughed at you. I'm sorry, please forgive me. My mind is all messed up. I have pictures of nude girls in my cell. My mind is all messed up. I wish I could talk to you. I wish they would let me. I wish you could pray for me."

I said, "I know you do. I do too, but I can't. I'll walk with you. Come on, I have to leave right now."

They already had told me when I went in there, "When you are talking to them, don't let over three of them get around you at a time. If as many as five or six get around you, there will be a cop there that will break it up. Don't talk to the same three or four prisoners over three or four minutes. We don't allow them to get into gangs, not even five or six of them. There are too many killings like that. You have to stay apart."

I said, "Okay, I'll watch it real close." So, I talked to him as we went over.

I have never been treated any nicer in my lifetime. When we got over there at the food, they had the highest respect for me. They treated me like their chaplain or something. They treated me so nice. Why?

Oh, yeah, that's really good Norvel. You really knew what to say, didn't you?

No, I didn't. You've got to be kidding. They made fun of me. They laughed at me. They heckled me. But the GIFT OF FAITH they didn't. The gift of faith came upon me and gave me power—the amount of power I needed to get the job done, right then.

I had a good time with them. Many of the prisoners got saved and had a good time. They learned something that day. I guess they learned a little bit from me, but they learned mostly from *the gift of faith.*

7

To Set the Captives Free

The gift of faith will operate through you sometimes for a demon-possessed person, especially if the demon-possessed person wants to be free. If he is crying out for help and wants to be free, it will operate through you. It did me one time.

A girl in our town, a Spirit-filled Christian girl, was hanging around with the wrong boys and started going to bed with them. You have to realize you are doing something wrong and stop it.

When you go to bed with someone and you are not married, you have to recognize it is wrong, and just cut it off. The Holy Ghost will witness to you that it's wrong, *so stop it.* You can't just keep on doing it. If you keep on doing something that's wrong, anything that's wrong, it causes a demon to come in and start taking over control.

She went a little bit too much, because she liked it. She got possessed with the demon of lust. It's one thing to like sex, and it's another thing to be possessed with a demon of lust.

Sex in marriage is beautiful, but you are not allowed to do it outside of marriage. If you start fooling around with it outside of marriage, you'll open the door to the devil, and a demon of lust will come in. If you keep on, he'll come in and take you over. You'll become a slave to it, and you'll have to break that power.

She was raised as a Spirit-filled Christian. She knew better, but she got in so far that she couldn't get out.

She'd tell herself everyday, "I'm not going to bed with this boy tonight. I'm not going to. I'm not going to!" She'd get out; she'd say she wasn't going to, but she would wind up doing it—every night.

The college found out about it and asked her to leave. She was 19 or 20 years old.

She started visiting churches, knocking on the church doors, and asking for help. You know how most pastors are: they're real nice, and they prayed for her. **But you don't pray for a demon-possessed person. You cast the devil out of them!**

There is a difference between praying a prayer, and casting a devil out. You have to break the power of the devil, if the devil's there.

To break the power of the devil you say, "In Jesus' name, come out! You're not going to wreck this girl. I'm not going to let you! NOT GOING TO LET YOU! You have no choice. I'm not going to give you any!"

Until a demon meets a man that doesn't give him any choice, then his choice is to make a slave out of that girl's body. That's his choice.

That's always a demon's choice: to make a slave out of your body for alcohol, dope, or anything it can get into you to destroy you. The devil is a slave driver. He'll drive you just like a slave. You won't have any choice. Not until you meet somebody that knows how to cast out devils. A person might have a good ministry, but unless he knows how to cast out devils he can't help that person, because they're demon possessed.

I was planning to go to a convention, I think in Kansas City. The Lord let me know that He didn't want me to go to the convention. He wanted me to go to a prayer meeting Wednesday night. The Lord said to me,

"Don't leave town, Son. Go to the prayer meeting Wednesday night at the church."

I said, "Okay, Lord."

I went to the prayer meeting on Wednesday night. There is never as big a crowd on Wednesday night as there is on Sunday. There were a few people there. The preacher preached and gave an invitation. One girl got up out of her seat and went down to the front altar. The Spirit of God said in me, "Go pray with her."

So I did. I went down and prayed with her. I got down on my knees beside her and prayed with her. She was crying out for help. She said, "Oh help me Jesus. Oh God help me, some way Lord, help me." I never heard such a cry. The people back in the congregation couldn't hear it, because she was crying with a little tiny voice.

She cried, "Help me Jesus. Some way help me Lord."

I thought to myself, what's wrong with her? I was praying, "Yeah, Jesus, help her. Help her Lord."

I was the only one up there praying. I prayed for about 15 minutes, I think. Right towards the end when I was praying, one or two more came up, knelt down around there and started praying. I felt I didn't want to pray any more. I got up off my knees and went back to my seat and sat down.

I was sitting there, minding my own business, and the Lord began to roll the 16th chapter of the book of Mark around in front of me—the Great Commission.

"Go ye into all the world, and preach the gospel to every creature. He that believeth and is baptized shall be saved; but he that believeth not shall be damned. And these signs shall follow them that believe; In my name shall they cast out devils." In my name they shall cast

out devils. In my name they shall cast out devils. In my name they shall cast out devils.

I said, "Yeah, Lord, I hear it. Please Lord, Jesus, in this particular church, I don't think they cast out devils."

"The 16th chapter of the book of Mark casts them out."

God doesn't go by your church. Is that a shock to you? Wherever you go to church, God doesn't go by church services; He goes by the Bible.

"Lord, I don't have enough power to do that," I said. "Don't make me do that. I have friends here. I don't think the pastor and his wife cast out devils. Besides that, Lord, I don't run this church, they do. I don't think they do that in here."

"The 16th chapter of the book of Mark does. In my NAME THEY SHALL CAST OUT DEVILS. Those that believe in me, in my name they shall cast out devils."

"Yes, Lord, yes." I was crying by that time. He just kept rolling it around in front of me, just like He had a one-track mind. I wanted the Lord to get over in the book of Matthew, or Luke, but He didn't go anywhere. He just stayed in the 16th chapter of the book of Mark and the Great Commission.

"These signs shall follow them that believe, in my name they shall cast out devils."

Yes, Lord, I know it's in there. I know it's in there," I said. All the time I was trying to talk to Him, He wasn't even listening.

After a while, I said, "Lord, I work for you."

"I know you do. I hear you going around the country saying that you love me, you love me, 'Oh, I love Jesus.

Jesus has done so much for me; let me tell you what He's done for me.' TONIGHT I DEMAND YOU SHOW ME!"

Words are cheap. I already knew what He wanted me to do, but I was trying to get out of it.

He started melting me. He said, *"Look at that girl at the altar, crying out for help. Look at her, Son. She's crying out for help and nobody has helped her. She's been to church, after church, after church and she's still crying out for help."*

That makes Jesus mad; when somebody comes to His church and cries out for help and nobody will help her. It's a wonder God doesn't give us a spanking. We're believers!

Jesus said, "LOOK AT HER! I want to help her, **through you.**"

This got me; I couldn't take it. I absolutely could not take it.

He said to me just so plainly, *"It doesn't make any difference to me now, the past is past. It doesn't make any difference to me how many boys she's been to bed with. I love her, and she's crying out for me. I love her, and I love all of those like her. If you are going to work for me, you better not forget that. I didn't put that evil spirit in her that makes her do the things she does. The devil put it in her. The devil has gotten in her. I want you to go up there and use my name, and cast that thing out of her."*

"Jesus," I said, "I don't have enough power to do it in a church where they don't even do it. I don't have enough power to do this in front of my friends. I don't have enough nerve or backbone or whatever you need to do it in a church that doesn't even do it. Lord, I'm not ashamed of you, Jesus."

"Show me. Son, you love me? Show me. If you are not ashamed of the 16th chapter of the book of Mark, you are not ashamed of me. If you are ashamed to obey it, you are ashamed of me. If you are not ashamed of me, and you love me, show me. I love her. I want to help her."

I said, "Jesus, you have the power. I know you have the power; go ahead and help her Lord."

"I work through my Word. I work through believers. I'll do what you do. You obey the 16th chapter of the book of Mark, and I'll be with you."

Remember what Jesus told the disciples? "I will go with you, confirming the Word with signs following." He didn't say, "I'll go BEFORE you and do all the work." He said, "I'll go WITH you, confirming the Word with signs FOLLOWING."

It was up to the disciples, and to you and me, to stick to the Word, and God comes and DOES the Bible.

"Give me power, Jesus," I said, "and I'll do it. I'll do anything you tell me to do, if you'll give me power." I meant business.

As soon as I said that, on the inside of my belly, the Holy Ghost began to rise up, like somebody blowing up a balloon. **The power began to come into me.** I had power in my fingers. I had power in my hands. I had power in my arms. I had power in my chest. I had power in my eyes. My eyes were full of power, I couldn't see anything except victory! My mouth was full of power! **Everything about me was full of power.**

When the power came on me, I got up out of my seat! I walked down there like I was going to battle. As I got down there, there was a guy standing there close to her.

"Have her stand up because God is going to set her free!" I said.

He said, "Stand up, young lady; stand up."

I put my hand on the side of her head and said, "**You foul spirit that has wrecked this girl's life, in Jesus' name, COME OUT OF HER!**" I SAID IT ONE TIME. It was like the wind. It had to be a demon—WHOOSH! Her body went back through the air, and hit the floor. She landed flat on her back. The moment she hit the floor tears gushed out of her eyes and she started speaking in tongues, just as fast as she could.

The *gift of faith* made the difference. It gave me power to get the job done. The people all shouted and rejoiced and praised God.

Several months later that pastor called me. The girl was going to get married. "She wants you to read the Bible at her wedding," he said.

I went there to read the Bible at her wedding. I was standing there at the wedding with the Bible in my hand. The pastor was standing beside me with a Bible. She got married in her house.

The wedding started. She was in the other room. She came around the corner, marching to *Here Comes The Birde*. I had the scripture all set that I was going to read to her. (She wanted me to have a part in her wedding, because the Lord used me to set her free.) She came around the corner, walking towards me. I looked and saw her.

The Spirit of the Lord came upon me, and so softly and sweetly Jesus spoke to me. Tears were streaming down my cheeks. He said, "Thank you, Son, for obeying the 16th chapter of the book of Mark and for casting the devil out of her. Now she comes to be married, and she stands before me, clean and white as snow. She stands before me as an angel, as though she had never sinned." Glory be to God!

Can you imagine Jesus thanking me for doing something? You know what it means for Jesus to come to you and thank you? I want to thank Him for what He has done for me.

Oh, praise the blessed name of the Lord God forever! Because of the gift of faith!

8

To Bring Salvation

Some people called me from Philadelphia, Pennsylvania and wanted me to come to a business meeting. They were introducing a product to the American market. God told me to go, so I flew to Philadelphia.

A big-shot, real educated type guy came out, and began to lecture, and show us the product; tell us how it would be distributed, and explain it to us. There were several businessmen from different parts of the country there. They were going to ask us questions about what we thought of it. I have been in the sales business, all my life, and they wanted to get my opinion on it, as well as a lot of other men's opinions.

We sat there; they asked us for our opinion about it, and we told them. I told them I didn't believe it would work, and it didn't. (They tried it, but it didn't work.)

Between the sessions, they dismissed us to go eat. We walked into a restaurant, and we didn't have any reservations. We walked over to the dining room. When they said, "Table for two," the man who was doing the lecturing and I just stepped out. We sat down at the table.

I'm a CHRISTIAN businessman. It's just a normal thing to me to sit down, and say, "Well, thank you Jesus. Praise the Lord. Isn't Jesus good?"

He looked at me, and said, "Mr. Hayes, I want to tell you something. I don't believe in that kind of stuff."

"What kind of stuff?" I asked.

"That Jesus business, or God business," he said. "I don't believe in that kind of stuff."

"You don't believe in God?"

"No!"

I thought, this is going to be a long dinner. If you have to eat with somebody, and you can't talk about Jesus, what are you going to talk about? I said, "Okay. He's real, but to each his own."

We just started talking about business, and other things. "You have been telling me several different things. I have a question I want to ask you that has been bugging me about you. I just want to ask you one question. Why don't you believe in God?"

He said, "People say that God is love."

"He is."

"Oh, yeah? My wife is an alcoholic, Mr. Hayes. I have a 12-year-old son and a 14-year-old son. My 14-year-old son is a dope addict. If God is love, He sure didn't stop at our house. Why should you believe in Him?"

I said, "You have to believe God. You have to show God faith that you believe in Him. God will give you whatever you want."

"You believe what you want to believe; I don't believe it. God could be real, but I don't believe it."

"He is," I told him. Then I started giving my testimony, telling him what God had done for me. It was like water running off a duck's back. He didn't believe a word of it.

"It may be true, but I doubt it. It probably just turned out that way for you. I don't believe it."

He let me know it didn't even phase him. We finished eating.

We were walking up the sidewalk to the meeting room. I was minding my own business, talking to him. Some of the other men were walking in front of us, and some were behind us.

All of a sudden, POWER fell on me and changed me into another man! He gave me words to say to him. When it happened to me, I just wheeled around; I got him by the arm and pulled him around. I stuck my finger in his face, and I said, **"Listen Mister, God's real regardless of what you believe! Jesus told me to tell you that He doesn't want your two sons to die and go to hell. If you don't introduce them to Him, when you die and go to hell, He's going to hold you responsible for them!"**

I just turned around and walked off. He stood there looking like I hit him with a stick.

I went in and sat over against the wall. He came and sat at the desk, because he was the lecturer. I looked over at him and the *gift of faith* came upon me again; POWER came upon me again. This time it was a different type of manifestation. The first time on the sidewalk was *authority*. This time the Spirit of God began to move upon my innermost being and I began to *cry* and *weep*. Compassion boiled up out of me. The power was all over me.

The Lord said to me, "Walk over there and pray for him, right now."

Some of the other men had come in and were sitting around.

I just walked across the floor crying. I walked up to his desk. I said, *"As I was sitting against the wall the Spirit of the Lord came upon me. Jesus loves you and He wants me to pray for you. Bow your head and close your eyes and I'm going to pray for you right now."* I was crying. He looked up at me and my hands were up.

43

He said, "Oh, oh, okay."

I reached up and touched him on the top of the head, and I said, *"Jesus, touch this man. Jesus, give this man another life. Touch him!"* His head fell down onto the desk like he'd been hit with a hammer. He started crying as soon as his head hit the desk; he started crying and weeping.

I said, "Tell Jesus you are sorry for your sin. Ask Jesus to come into your heart, Mister, right now. The Spirit of the Lord is all over you. Ask Him to come into your heart!"

He said, "Jesus, come into my heart." He just cried and wept and sobbed on the top of the desk. There he was, five minutes ago, he didn't believe in God.

You might say, "Norvel, that was a good job. You really did the right thing, didn't you."

Are you kidding? I told him everything I knew and it didn't phase him. My knowledge of God couldn't even get to him. **It was a gift of power that God gave that made the difference.**

A year later I was sitting in a FGBMFI convention in Phoenix, Arizona on the stage. I saw a guy walking up the aisle grinning from ear to ear. He jumped up on the stage where I was sitting. (The service hadn't started yet. There were about 3,000 people in attendance.) He walked over to me and said, "Brother Norvel, it's wonderful. God is wonderful. Jesus is wonderful."

"Yeah, I know He is. I know He is wonderful."

"Don't you remember me—Philadelphia, Pennsylvania?" he asked.

"Oh, dear Lord! Yeah, I remember you."

"Do you know what happened to me?"

"No."

"I went home to my alcoholic wife," he said. "I told her 'I met this strange man. He put his hands on my head and something came in me and knocked me on the desk. I began to cry and weep.' I told her that I got saved. Then she got saved. I told my dope-addict son, and he got saved. My son got filled with the Holy Ghost. I got filled with the Holy Ghost. My wife got filled with the Holy Ghost. My wife is here. My son is going to Bible school, all my relatives are saved. I moved from Philadelphia to California. I'm the president of a FGBMFI chapter in California now."

I said, "You mean all in one year?"

"It doesn't take me long to do something," he said.

See, God wanted to save him. You might say, "Why did God save him?"

Because I was available for the gift to operate through. The gift of faith came upon me! The power was on me. The power went from me into him when I touched him on the top of his head. The gift of faith can change people. The Spirit of God can change people through the gift of faith. But He has to have believers to operate through.

It's a supernatural gift! It's available for the Church. It's available for you—anybody! It makes up the difference. That's the reason you've got to have it. You need it, because He'll manifest himself, and He'll make the difference.

But the gift of faith will never operate through you unless you make yourself available.

You have to make yourself available. You have to do your best to get your spirit in the condition that Paul got his spirit.

Paul said, "For I am not ashamed of the gospel of Christ: for it is the power of God unto salvation to everyone that believeth; to the Jew first, and also to the Greek" (Romans 1:16).

"But I keep under my body, and bring it into subjection: lest that by any means, when I have preached to others, I myself should be a castaway" (I Corinthians 9:27).

"I have fought a good fight, I have finished my course, I have kept the faith" (II Timothy 4:7).

Don't let your body control you so that you're ashamed of anything where the gospel is concerned. Pray and fast until you get your body under subjection, so that you're not ashamed anymore. Pray in tongues until the fire of God comes and burns it out of you.

Make yourself available for the gift of faith. Tell Jesus that you are available.

Say: "Jesus, I'm available for the gift of faith. I'm available to be changed into another person: to help somebody, to bring healing to somebody, to bring salvation to somebody, to stop the evil works of the devil, and to bring the glory of God into manifestation on the earth. I'm available for God's power to come upon me and change me. I'm available.

"I love you Jesus. I love the gospel. Mold me into the person you want me to be. I believe in I Corinthians chapter 12. I believe the gift of faith is a gift of power that God gives to believers to get the job done. Thank you Jesus, I'm free from unbelief."